PETS' GUIDES

Beaky's Guide to

Caring for Your Birds

Isabel Thomas

Raintree is an imprint of Capstone Global Library Limited, a company incorporated in England and Wales having its registered office at 7 Pilgrim Street, London, EC4V 6LB – Registered company number: 6695582

www.raintreepublishers.co.uk
myorders@raintreepublishers.co.uk

Text © Capstone Global Library Limited 2015
First published in hardback in 2014
The moral rights of the proprietor have been asserted.

Edited by James Benefield and Brynn Baker
Designed by Cynthia Akiyoshi
Picture research by Tracy Cummins
Production by Victoria Fitzgerald
Originated by Capstone Global Library Limited
Printed and bound in China by RR Donnelley Asia

ISBN 978-1-406-28175-0

18 17 16 15 14
10 9 8 7 6 5 4 3 2 1

British Library Cataloguing in Publication Data
A full catalogue record for this book is available from the British Library.

Acknowledgements
We would like to thank the following for permission to reproduce photographs: Alamy: © Marmaduke St. John, 19; Capstone Library: Karon Dubke, 7, 11, 12, 14, 20, 23, 26; Getty Images: Andreas Arnold, 5; Shutterstock: Edoma, 9, Sarycheva Olesia, 16; Superstock: Belinda Images, 24, imagebroker.net, front cover; Design Elements Shutterstock: iBird, Picsfive, R-studio.

We would like to thank Les Rance for his assistance in the preparation of this book.

Every effort has been made to contact copyright holders of material reproduced in this book. Any omissions will be rectified in subsequent printings if notice is given to the publisher.

All the Internet addresses (URLs) given in this book were valid at the time of going to press. However, due to the dynamic nature of the Internet, some addresses may have changed, or sites may have changed or ceased to exist since publication. While the author and publisher regret any inconvenience this may cause readers, no responsibility for any such changes can be accepted by either the author or the publisher.

Contents

Some words are shown in bold, **like this**. You can find out what they mean by looking in the glossary.

Do you want pet birds?

G'day! I'm Beaky the budgie, and this book is all about birds like me! Did you know that some birds make great pets? Our colourful feathers and happy birdsong will brighten up your home. Some of us can even talk to you!

Before getting a pet bird, be sure you can look after me properly. I'll need a safe, clean place to live, food and water, things to play with, company, and **vet** care if I get sick or injured. Care for me well and I'll quickly become your best friend!

Choosing your birds

Budgies like me are the most popular pet birds. I'm not surprised – we're beautiful! Cockatiels, zebra finches and canaries also make great family pets. Some birds will happily hop on to your hand or sit on your shoulder. Others do not like to be handled.

I feel lonely when I'm kept on my own. If you would like to keep budgies or zebra finches, buy at least two birds. Then we'll always have company. It's best to get two boy birds or two girl birds.

Before you buy a bird, ask where it came from. I am happy to live with people because I was born in **captivity**. Never buy or keep birds that have been taken from the wild.

Me when I was little

Animal shelters and **rescue centres** are the best places to get new pets. You can also buy birds at pet shops or from a good **breeder**. It is best to choose young birds, or birds that are already **hand tamed**.

Getting ready

Now it's time to go shopping. Make sure you have everything you need before you bring me home. I can't sleep in your bed! I need plenty of space to stretch my wings and to keep fit by flying. My dream home is an **aviary**.

Pet birds can also be kept in a wire cage.
Make sure you choose the largest one
possible. Different types of birds need different
cages. Ask a vet or a bird expert for advice. If
the bars are too far apart, your new pet could
escape. They could also get their beak, wings
or feet trapped.

Don't forget the furniture! Pet birds need several **perches** at different heights. Look for specially cleaned tree branches in pet shops. I'll also need lots of toys, so I never get bored. You don't have to wait until it's my birthday!

Beaky's budgie shopping list:

- an aviary or wire cage
- perches the right size for my feet
- budgie food
- food and water containers
- paper to line the bottom of my cage
- special bird toys

13

Welcome home

Moving can be scary, especially for birds. Help me settle in by picking the perfect place for my cage. My favourite spot is the corner of a warm, light room. I'll enjoy watching you play, but I'll also feel safe.

Please don't
put my cage:

X Next to a window. I don't like **draughts** or
bright sunshine.

X Near a radiator or heater.

X On the floor.

X Near a TV or radio.

X In or near the kitchen. Cooking **fumes** can
make me ill.

X In a room where strong-smelling things like
hairspray, perfume, glue or paints are used.

X In a room where somebody smokes.

Feeding time

You can buy special bird food from pet shops. Pellets are like a perfect packed lunch, and they help me to stay healthy. Ask for help to choose my food. I need fresh, cold water to drink all the time. Also, seeds make a delicious treat!

Budgies can't eat all fruit and vegetables. Check out the list on page 28. However, I like to nibble fresh food every day. How about making it a game by hiding small pieces of fruit and vegetables in my cage? Wash everything well and take out any pips.

Cleaning my home

I need a clean home to stay healthy. I can't clean out my cage, so I'm relying on you! Clear away **stale** food, and wash out my water container every day. Change the paper at the bottom of my cage to get rid of any droppings.

You will need to **disinfect** the whole cage every week. Remember to clean my toys and perches, too. Perches made from tree branches can be replaced if they get too dirty to wipe clean.

Handling and exercise

Cockatiels and budgies can learn to perch on your hand. Start by putting your hand in our cage to offer a tasty treat. Move slowly and quietly so I don't get frightened. Next, try holding out a perch or finger for me to hop on to.

When I am hand-tamed, let me out of my
cage every day. Pet birds need to exercise
by flying around a safe room. Keep windows
and doors closed, and watch me carefully
so I don't nibble anything dangerous. Cover
windows and mirrors so I don't fly into them
by mistake. Ouch!

Grooming and care

I need a bath every day to keep my feathers clean. Give me a bowl of shallow water and I'll do the hard work! You can even give pet birds a shower by spraying clean water from a **mister**.

Just like your fingernails, my beak never stops growing. Chewing special wooden toys will stop my beak from getting too long. Please don't let me nibble painted wood, furniture or your toys. They could poison me.

Visiting the vet

Take me to visit a vet when I first come to live with you. I'll need a check-up every year. The vet can help you to care for me, make sure I'm healthy, and trim my beak and nails.

Birds can't tell you when they feel sick. If you spot any of these illness signs, take me to the vet right away:

- I've fluffed up my feathers
- I'm quiet or sleepy
- I'm fatter or thinner than usual
- I'm eating or drinking less than usual
- my droppings are runny
- I'm sneezing or coughing
- I'm limping
- my beak or eyes are crusty

Holiday care

When you go on holiday, ask a friend or neighbour to visit me every day. They'll need to fill my food and water, and keep my cage clean. Tell them what illness signs to look out for.

We are best friends now, so I'll miss you while you're away. Remember to tell me all about your holiday when you get back. I love it when you talk to me. I might even start to chatter back!

Budgie facts

- The proper name for budgies is budgerigars.

- The first budgies came from Australia.

- Wild budgies are always green and yellow.

- Pet budgies can be hundreds of different colours and patterns.

- Pet budgies can live for up to 15 years. Most live for about 8 years.

- Rhubarb, avocado and chocolate are poisonous to budgies.

- Like all birds, budgies are scared of animals like cats and dogs. A pet bird might not be a good choice if you already have other pets.

Beaky's top tips

- Choose lots of toys for your pet birds, and swap them around so we don't get bored. We like swings, ladders and mirrors for **preening**. We enjoy toys we can chew or ones with bells or chimes.

- Try making your own bird toys. Use safe materials such as cardboard tubes, dried pasta, lolly sticks and clean shoelaces.

- Don't worry if I try to tear my toys apart – it's part of the fun!

- Play with me lots. You can even teach me games such as climbing your fingers, hide-and-seek or ringing a bell.

- Seeds and popcorn are special treats. But I shouldn't have them too often because they are fattening!

Glossary

animal shelter place for animals that have no home

aviary room-sized cage for keeping birds in

breeder person who helps animals to have babies in an organized way

captivity kept by humans instead of living in the wild

disinfect clean something with special chemicals to kill harmful germs

draught cool breeze inside a building from an open door or window

fume any gas or vapour that has a strong smell or is dangerous to breathe in

hand-tamed used to being handled

mister bottle with a spray attached to create a mist

perch when a bird rests on something, or the object they rest on

preen when a bird cleans its feathers using its beak

rescue centre organization that rescues animals that are lost, injured or not being taken care of properly

stale not fresh and not good to eat

vet person trained to care for sick or injured animals

Find out more

Books

How to Look After Your Budgie, David Alderton (Armadillo Books, 2014)

Pets Plus: Birds, Sally Morgan (Franklin Watts, 2013)

Websites

www.budgerigarsociety.com
The Budgerigar Society can help you to find breeders and bird clubs in your area.

www.pdsa.org.uk/pet-health-advice/budgerigars
The PDSA website has advice about caring for pet budgerigars.

Index